Hints and tips

•When you look for things in the garden, be careful not to tread on any plants.

•Try to look at creatures without disturbing them. If you do move them, always return them to the place where you found them.

•Before touching soil, always cover any cuts with a plaster.

•Do not rub your face or eyes when working with plants or soil.

Wherever you see this sign, ask an adult to help you. Never use sharp tools or go exploring on your own.

Get an adult to help you

BE CAREFUL NOT TO PICK UP SHARP THINGS

This warning sign shows where you have to take special care when doing the project. For example, when looking for nest-building materials, you must be careful not to pick up any sharp objects. They may hurt you or the birds.

Wheel of life

Life cycles are made up of the stages that all living things go through as they grow and develop. Build a wheel of life to show how a living thing starts its life then grows into an adult that can start another new life.

Life cycle wheel

1 You will need two pieces of coloured card. Draw round a plate to make two circles and cut them out.

Get an adult to help you

2 Use a ruler to draw lines from top to bottom and side to side on one of the circles. This divides it into quarters. On the other circle, cut out a window. Decorate the rest of the circle.

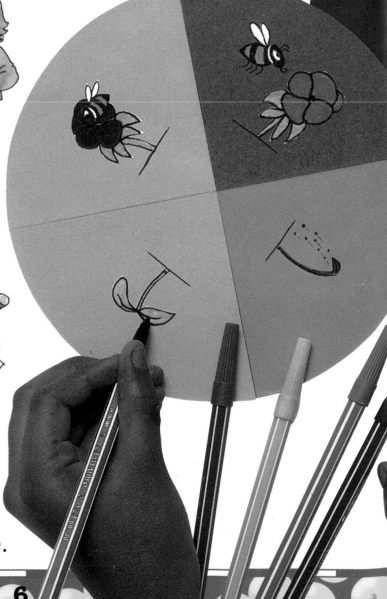

Contents

Introduction

Animals and plants are alive, so we call them living things. All living things go through a life cycle. You can have fun learning about the stages in different life cycles. Record how you change and grow, and watch a potato shoot grow up through a maze.

1 Look out for numbers like this. They will guide you through the step-by-step instructions for the projects and activities, making sure that you do things in the right order.

Further facts

Whenever you see this 'nature spotters' sign, you will find interesting information to help you understand more about life cycles. For example, read about how long different animals live.

Life Cycles

Sally Hewitt

Franklin Watts
London • Sydney

An Aladdin Book
© Aladdin Books Ltd 2000
Produced by
Aladdin Books Ltd
28 Percy Street
London W1P OLD

First published in Great Britain
in 2000 by
Franklin Watts Books
96 Leonard Street
London EC2A 4XD

ISBN 0-7496-3715-3 (hardcover)
ISBN 0-7496-4610-1 (paperback)

Editor: Kathy Gemmell

Consultant: Helen Taylor

Designer: Simon Morse

Photography: Roger Vlitos

Illustrators: Tony Kenyon, Stuart Squires – SGA
& Mike Atkinson

Original concept by David West Children's Books

3 In each quarter, draw a picture of one stage of the life cycle of a living thing. This wheel shows the life cycle of a flower called a pansy.

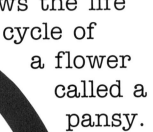

• A bee lands on a pansy.

• The bee carries pollen to another pansy.

• The pansy makes seeds, dies, and the seeds fall to the ground.

• A new pansy plant shoots up.

4 Join the circles at the centre with a paper fastener. Turn the top circle clockwise to watch your wheel go round. Make more wheels to show other life cycles.

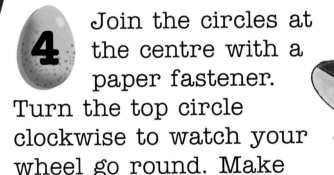

Pollen and seeds

A flower like a pansy makes new seeds when a bee rubs pollen from another pansy onto it.

The pollen rubs off the bee onto a part of the flower called the stigma. From there, it moves down inside the flower to the ovary, where the new seeds are made.

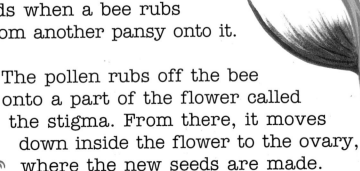

Pollen

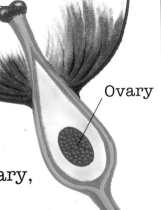

Stigma

Ovary

Reproduction

For life to go on, living things must reproduce. This means they must make a new baby or plant like themselves. New life usually begins in an egg inside a mother's body. The egg can start to grow when a seed from a male joins it.

WASH YOUR HANDS AFTER TOUCHING RAW EGG

Inside a hen's egg

1 Crack open a hen's egg onto a white plate. Try not to break the yolk. The shell protects the delicate insides.

A red spot inside the yolk is the growing baby chick, called an embryo.

Eggs

Many animals lay eggs. Some time later, the eggs hatch. Other baby creatures grow inside their mother's body.

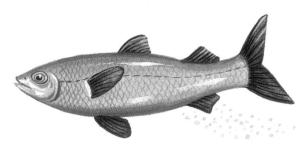

Fish lay a great number of eggs. The eggs float in the water and many are eaten by hungry sea creatures.

Female insects lay tiny eggs and leave them to hatch on their own.

Birds build nests to lay their eggs in. The mother and father birds often take turns to keep the eggs warm and safe.

People and many other animals don't lay eggs. Instead, the egg is inside the mother. When seed called sperm from the father joins the egg, a new baby starts to grow. It grows inside the mother until it is ready to be born.

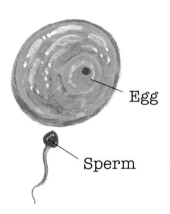

Egg

Sperm

The yellow yolk is food for the embryo.

The egg white is like a cushion around the embryo.

2 Look at the insides of the egg. The egg is full of food for the growing chick. Now cook and eat the egg.

Growing up

It takes many years for a human baby to become an adult. You have grown and changed a great deal since the day you were born. You will stop growing one day but you will never stop changing and learning.

Life scrapbook

1 Stick a picture of you as a baby into a scrapbook. Write down how much you weighed.

2 Ask a friend to draw round your feet on paper. Cut out the shapes and stick them into your scrapbook.

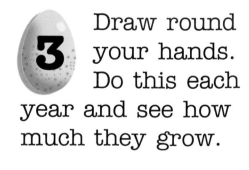

3 Draw round your hands. Do this each year and see how much they grow.

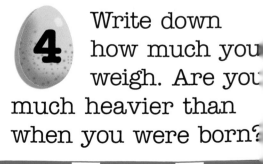

4 Write down how much you weigh. Are you much heavier than when you were born?

Big and small

All animals grow from babies to adults. Some grow much faster than others.

Elephants

An elephant can live for 75 years. A baby stays with its mother for up to ten years.

Mice

After only three weeks, baby mice have to leave their nest to look for their own food.

Parrots

Parrots can live for a very long time. Some have lived to be 80 years old.

5 Stick a long piece of paper to a wall. Ask a friend to mark how tall you are. A year later, do the same and see how much you have grown.

Mayflies

Mayflies are born, live their life and die all in one day. They have one of the shortest lifetimes of any creature.

Food for growth

You need to eat food from four food groups every day. Proteins help you grow and keep you healthy. Fats keep you warm. Carbohydrates give you energy and keep you going. Fruit and vegetables are full of vitamins.

Lunch boxes

1 Make sure that you pack your lunch box with a healthy meal. Cheese and ham in your sandwiches will give you protein and some fat. Bread will give you carbohydrate.

2 Cheese, yoghurt and butter are all made from milk. They give you protein and some fat. You should also drink plenty of water every day.

Carnivores and herbivores

Animals eat different kinds of food. Animals that eat meat are called carnivores. Animals that just eat plants are called herbivores.

A tiger is a carnivore. It hunts and kills its prey for food.

Sheep are herbivores. They graze on grass.

Ladybirds are carnivores. They feed on tiny bugs called aphids. Aphids suck juice called sap from plants.

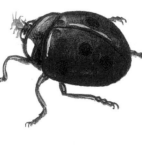

3 Fruit and vegetables give you vitamins, minerals and roughage. Roughage helps your food to pass easily through your body.

A giraffe is a herbivore. It stretches its long neck to reach up to eat leaves from tall trees.

4 A lot of salt and sugar is not good for you, so don't pack too many sweet biscuits and salty snacks.

Plants and seeds

A bean is a kind of seed that you find inside a bean pod. Plant a bean from a packet and watch it grow into a new bean plant. Look carefully at the different stages the bean goes through.

Plant a bean

1 You will need cotton wool, a glass jar and beans from a packet.

2 Soak the beans in water overnight to soften their tough skin. Line the jar with cotton wool. Pour in water until the cotton wool is damp but not soaking wet.

3 Space the beans around the edge of the jar. Put the jar on a windowsill. Dampen the cotton wool every day.

4 After a few days, the beans will begin to sprout. Make a diary of how they grow. Watch how the roots grow down before the shoots begin to grow up.

Life cycle of a flowering plant

The life cycle of a nasturtium flower follows the same pattern as many other flowering plants.

Spring is the time for seeds under the earth to start growing.

A shoot pushes through the earth towards the light.

In warm weather, flowers bloom. Insects feed on a sweet juice made by the flower called nectar.

Frost kills the plant and its seeds fall into the earth, where they rest until spring.

Growing plants

Plants need sunlight, water, air and goodness from the soil to be able to make their own food and to grow. Without even one of these, the plant will not be strong and healthy and may even die. Find out what happens to a plant without sunlight, water or air.

Happy plants

1 You will need four young plants. Water the first one. Leave it in an airy place in sunlight. Watch how well it grows.

2 Put the second plant next to the first, but don't water it. It will soon start to wilt.

3 Water the third plant, but put a box over it. The green will fade and the plant will begin to die.

Plant survival

Plants have found ways of surviving in all corners of the Earth.

Desert plants have long roots. These search for water which is stored in the fleshy stems.

Rainforest creepers with shiny leaves climb up the tall trees towards the sunlight.

Mountain plants grow close to the ground or in cracks away from cold winds.

4 Spread petroleum jelly on a leaf of the last plant so that air can't get to it. Watch the leaf shrivel after a few days.

Growing without seeds

Some plants can grow new plants without seeds. A potato is a root that is packed with the food that the new potato plant needs in order to grow. It has little buds called eyes.

A potato maze

1 You can grow a new potato plant from an old potato. You will need a potato with eyes, a shoe box with a lid, card, scissors and tape.

Get an adult to help you

2 Cut three strips of card for the maze and make a hole in one end of the box.

3 Bend the end of each strip of card to make a flap. Tape the flaps to the sides of the box.

4 Place the potato in the box and put on the lid. After a few days, shoots will start to grow from the eyes up through the maze towards the light.

Light

New plants from old plants

New plants can start to grow from parts of old plants.

A new garlic plant will grow from a piece of a garlic bulb.

You can grow a new African violet plant from a leaf planted in soil.

Strawberry plants grow long stems called runners. New little plants grow along the runners.

A piece of a geranium plant will grow roots if you put it in water or plant it.

Shoots will grow from a carrot top if you put it in water.

Birds

All birds lay eggs. Most birds build a nest to keep their eggs safe and warm until they hatch. Put out some materials in spring and see which ones a bird will choose to build its nest.

Bird box

1 Ask an adult to make or buy a strong bird box. Fix it firmly to a tree where it is safe from cats.

2 Collect materials like straw, cotton wool, dry leaves, hay, feathers, wool, shredded paper or even hair from a hairbrush.

3 Spread your materials on the ground around the nesting box. See which ones the birds choose. Birds mostly use natural materials like sticks, leaves, mud and moss to build their nests.

4 Watch the birds carry the materials into the nesting box. Some may take the nesting materials to build a nest nearby.

Life cycle of a blue tit

Like all birds, a blue tit begins its life inside an egg.

The adult bird keeps the egg warm until it hatches.

The egg hatches into a hungry baby bird called a nestling.

The young bird begins to look for its own food and learns to fly. It is now a fledgling.

It can soon manage without help from its mother and father.

The adult bird finds a mate. The female lays eggs in the spring.

Newts and snakes

Newts, frogs and toads all belong to a group of animals called amphibians. They lay their eggs, called spawn, in water. Baby amphibians live underwater. As adults, they live in water and on land. Reptiles, like snakes, have scaly skins and lay eggs.

Life cycle of a newt

1 A female newt lays hundreds of eggs on underwater plants. The eggs are surrounded by jelly.

2 Baby newts begin to grow inside the eggs. They feed on the jelly until they hatch out as tadpoles.

3 Newt tadpoles have gills to let them breathe underwater, like fish. They grow lungs to let them breathe air and they also grow legs

4 Adult newts live on land. They only go back into the water to keep their skin wet and to lay eggs.

Life cycle of a snake

1 Snakes are reptiles. They lay their eggs on the ground and then leave the eggs to hatch by themselves.

2 Newly hatched snakes are called hatchlings. They look just like tiny adult snakes.

4 Snakes grow and shed their skin all their lives. Adult snakes lay eggs and a new life cycle begins.

3 As snakes grow, they shed their skin. This means they grow new skin, wriggle out of the old skin and leave it behind in one piece.

Other reptile eggs

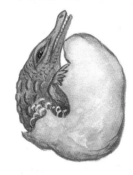

Crocodiles lay their eggs in sand. When they hatch, the mother carries them in her mouth to the water.

Mother turtles bury their eggs in the sand then swim away. The hatchlings make their own way down to the sea.

Butterflies

Some creatures change shape as they become adults. Tadpoles become frogs and caterpillars become butterflies. This change of shape is called metamorphosis. Find a caterpillar eating leaves. You may be able to follow its metamorphosis into a butterfly.

2 Caterpillars hatch out and feed on the leaves where the eggs were laid.

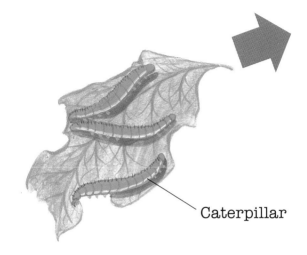

Caterpillar

Life cycle of a butterfly

1 The male butterfly finds a female butterfly to mate with. After mating, the female lays her eggs on a leaf, then flies off.

Eggs

3 Each caterpillar hangs by a silk thread and turns into a chrysalis. Inside the chrysalis, amazing changes take place.

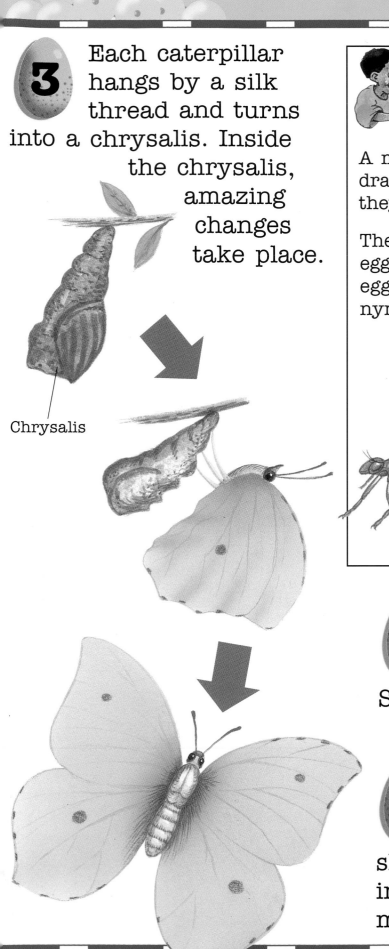

Chrysalis

Dragonfly

A dragonfly is another insect that changes shape.

A male and a female dragonfly mate as they fly through the air.

The female lays her eggs underwater. The eggs hatch into nymphs.

A nymph spends a year underwater. It climbs a reed, splits its skin and comes out as a dragonfly.

4 A butterfly struggles out of the chrysalis, dries its wings in the Sun and flies away.

5 Butterflies often live for only a short time. They have an important job to do. They must start a new life cycle.

Food web

All living things depend on the Sun. Plants use the Sun's energy to make their food. Herbivores eat plants, and carnivores eat the plant-eaters. Make a food web to see how life on Earth is linked together.

Weave a web

1 Think of animals that live near each other to put in your food web. Draw or cut out pictures of them from magazines.

2 Draw and cut out pictures of air, water, the Sun and some plants. Glue all of your pictures onto folded strips of card.

Get an adult to help you

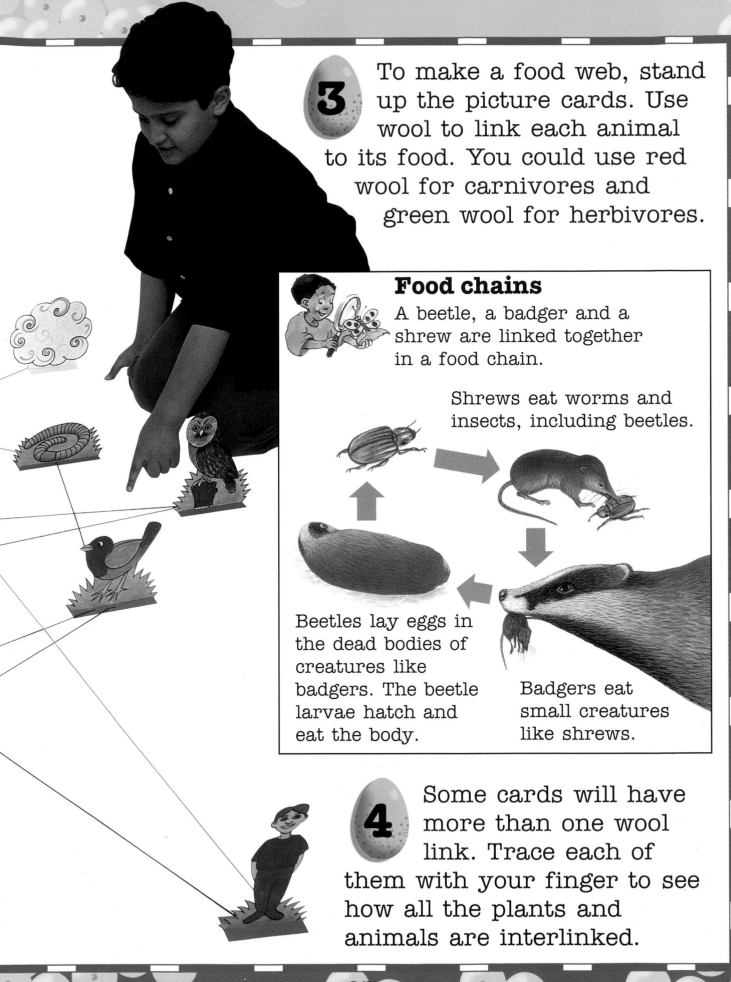

3 To make a food web, stand up the picture cards. Use wool to link each animal to its food. You could use red wool for carnivores and green wool for herbivores.

Food chains

A beetle, a badger and a shrew are linked together in a food chain.

Shrews eat worms and insects, including beetles.

Beetles lay eggs in the dead bodies of creatures like badgers. The beetle larvae hatch and eat the body.

Badgers eat small creatures like shrews.

4 Some cards will have more than one wool link. Trace each of them with your finger to see how all the plants and animals are interlinked.

Cycle of matter

When plants and animals die, they become part of the soil, making it full of the goodness plants need in order to grow. Study a pile of leaves to see how they rot down.

Rotting leaves

1 You will need strong gloves, a magnifying glass, a notebook and pencil and a pile of leaves.

WEAR GLOVES TO TOUCH ROTTING THINGS

2 Look at the leaves on the top of the pile. Now carefully spread them out. How are the top leaves different from the bottom ones?

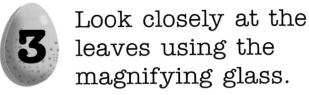

Falling leaves

When dead leaves fall, the goodness in them does not go to waste.

In the colder autumn weather, leaves lose their green colour and turn brown.

The leaves die and fall to the ground. Dry leaves crumble and wet leaves become soggy.

Gradually, the leaves become part of the soil around the tree.

The soil is made rich by the dead leaves. Seeds fall from the trees and grow well in this good soil.

3 Look closely at the leaves using the magnifying glass. Make a note of any creatures you spot. You might see beetles, worms, woodlice or millipedes.

Glossary

Amphibians

Amphibians are animals such as newts that lay their eggs underwater. The young animals live underwater. When they grow into adults, they live both underwater and on land.

Learn about the life cycle of a newt on page 22.

Beans

A bean is a kind of seed. Beans sprout the shoots and roots of a new bean plant.

Learn how to grow your own beans on pages 14-15.

Carbohydrates

Carbohydrates in food give us energy and help us to keep going. They are found in foods like bread and pasta.

Find out about the carbohydrates in your lunch box on pages 12-13.

Carnivores

Carnivores are animals that eat meat. They hunt and kill other animals for food.

Map out what carnivores eat in the project on pages 26-27.

Egg

An egg is where new life starts. People and some animals keep eggs inside their body. Birds and fish lay their eggs. A bird's egg contains the food the young bird needs before it hatches.

Find out about the insides of a hen's egg on pages 8-9.

Growing plants

Plants start new life from seeds, bulbs or other parts of the plant. New plants need sunlight, air, water and good soil to grow.

See what happens to plants that do not have these things on pages 16-17.

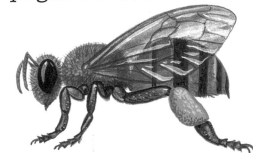

Herbivores

Herbivores are animals that eat plants or parts of plants such as nuts and berries. They are often eaten by carnivores.

Learn about some herbivores and carnivores on page 13.

Metamorphosis

Metamorphosis is what happens to an animal that changes shape as it grows, such as a caterpillar changing into a butterfly.

Learn about the metamorphosis of a butterfly on pages 24-25.

Pollen

Pollen is the yellow dust inside a flower. Insects carry pollen from one flower to another.

Turn to pages 6-7 to find out how flowers use pollen to make seeds.

Proteins

Proteins in food help us to grow and to keep healthy. They are found in foods such as meat, cheese and eggs.

Find out about proteins on pages 12-13.

Reproduction

For life to continue, all living things must make baby animals or new plants. This is called reproduction. Plants reproduce from seeds or from another part of the plant. Animals reproduce when a seed from a male joins an egg from a female and a new life begins.

Learn how animals reproduce on pages 8-9.

Reptiles

Reptiles are animals that lay eggs and have a scaly, waterproof skin. Some reptiles, such as snakes, live on land. Others, such as crocodiles, live mostly in water.

Learn about the life cycle of snakes, crocodiles and turtles on page 23.

Index

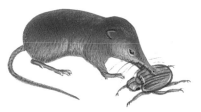

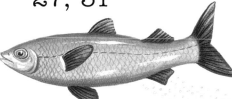

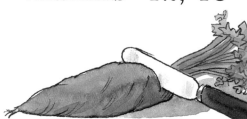